Buenos Aires.

A city to fall in love with, and fall in love in, the boulevards of the "Paris of South America" were modelled on the French capital. Waves of immigrants wove the social fabric, including vast numbers of Italians, Spanish, Jewish refugees, Armenians, and countless others. Throw in decades of immigration from Latin Americans seeking a better life and the resulting mix is intoxicating, and at times, vitriolic.

But all tension dissolves in the luscious aroma of beef grilling on the parrilla, the magnetic dust of dark tango bars, the crumbling façades of faded, palazzo-style buildings, and the personality of the people—whose flair for melodrama is matched only by their unparalleled wit.

Here, some local legends share their side of Buenos Aires. A world-famous Argentine chef, an ingenious fashion designer, a respected curator, the editors of a satirical magazine and a passionate tango singer. A feature explores the city on two wheels, a photo showcase plays on Argentine cultural stereotypes and a short story depicts a surreal romance. Get lost in the sights, sounds and flavours of the city. Get lost in Buenos Aires.

Photo: Rogério Tomaz Jr

The *Bosques de Palermo* (Palermo Woods)—officially Parque 3 de Febrero—
were part of the grounds of 19th-century dictator Juan Manuel de Rosas. After
his overthrow, the area was re-formed into the pleasure quarters it remains
today. The lone slice of modernism in its verdant space is *Planetario Galileo
Galilei* (pictured), completed in 1966. Architect Enrique Jan aimed to represent
human evolution—though it also calls to mind an alien landing pod. Stop in for
a show—in Spanish—or enjoy a transcendent backdrop to your sunny picnic.
• Planetario Galileo Galilei, Bosques de Palermo, Palermo, planetario.gob.ar

Speaking in Tongues

These days the legendary Buenos Aires dance music scene finds itself pegged back by draconian restrictions. That's why places like *Cocoliche* are more relevant than ever. The hardcore techno cave offers a glimpse of true underground, with varied local talent alongside international cult heroes. Saturdays tend to four-to-the-floor bangers, while housier Fridays are easier for the uninitiated. The club shares a name with the blend of Italian and Spanish—the uniquely charming dialect of the porteños.
• Cocoliche, Avenida Rivadavia 878, Centro

From Luxe Leather to Harbour Art

Ciudad de la Furia

Culture   Locos por el Fútbol

While the colourful, claustrophobic and edgy stands of *La Bombonera* (La Boca), home to Boca Junior's faithful, might be unrivalled, there are plenty of other famous stadiums worth visiting in Buenos Aires. More than a dozen teams here play in the top division and the fans are no less passionate. Boca's nemesis River Plate boast Argentina's biggest stadium, *El Monumental* in Núñez (pictured). Smaller but no less buzzing are the homes of clubs Vélez Sarsfield and Independiente: *Estadio José Amalfitani* (Liniers) and *Estadio Libertadores* (Avellaneda).
• Various locations, see Index p.60

Outdoors   Isle Love

The caramel rivers of the Tigre Delta wind between forested islands, like some prehistoric, sub-tropical Venice. The starting point is the town of Tigre, amazingly under an hour's ride from the diesel fumes of downtown Buenos Aires. To get there, take the commuter train from Retiro to Tigre, or change at Mitre station onto the scenic Tren de la Costa. Tigre's charms include the confusingly named crafts fair the *Puerto de Frutos*, and *Tigre Art Museum*, in an iconic former social club. There are also sights like the *Club de*

Regatas la Marina (pictured), illustrating almost a century and a half of boating activity. But it's the river-bus from Tigre's *Estación Fluvial* that takes you into another world. Some islands have hotels, country clubs and spa resorts. On others, rundown houses make a perfect set for a budget horror movie. But the best way to experience the Delta is to go rogue and rent a cottage. Take a crate of wine and plenty of meat—and an Argentine friend to do it justice on the grill.

• Tigre, various locations, see Index p.60

Shop Made in the South

When it comes to design, the sheer breadth in Buenos Aires is unrivalled on the continent. It's not strange to see flocks of foreign fashionistas roaming Palermo on shopping sprees—the city is a consumerist destination for the region. For those short on time, both *Panorama* and *Patrón* offer an extra-curated selection of wares for the home as well as limited-run clothing and accessories by independent designers. Panorama's vibrant interior (pictured) is a testament to the owner's youthful eye; find products from cult local names like Julieta Grana and Dubié. Laura Patrón Costas, meanwhile, has put together a rustic-chic sampling of handmade jewellery and luxe leather goods by local master artisans, herself included. The bijouterie is artfully displayed alongside pottery and one-off clothing items, making it a one-stop-shop for the pragmatic consumer.

• Panorama, República de la India 2905, Palermo, pnrm.com.ar; Patrón, Malabia 1644, Palermo, patronba.com

Food · Shop Open House

Sitting comfortably in the cushiest neighbourhood, *Casa Cavia* is a seriously civilised break from the big bad metropolis. The cultural centre is home to a patisserie, perfume shop, flower boutique, restaurant and publishing house—the spoils of which you can enjoy from the peaceful indoor patio. Time seems to slow down in this restored turn-of-the-century stunner. After all the last thing you need, while you decide on a bespoke scent or sample the cooking of star chef Pablo Massey, is to be in a rush.

• Casa Cavia, Cavia 2985, Recoleta, casacavia.com

Mouthful of Art

As the port which received the immigrants who built the city, La Boca hints at early Buenos Aires. The barrio isn't the safest, but rich culture lies beyond the "Caminito" tourist path with its street tango and brightly coloured houses. *Fundación Proa* (pictured) comprises four galleries, with a beautiful terrace upon the river. *Usina del Arte* is notable for its situation in a former power plant. And *Isla Flotante* co-curates with local artists. But don't leave La Boca without eating at *El Obrero*—for parrilla, pasta, and walls coated in football memorabilia. Order a taxi home.
• La Boca, various locations, see Index p.60

Food   Parrilla Paradise

Steakhouses dot this carniverous mecca. And serious meaters should leave the tourist zone for *El Ferroviario* (Liniers), a former football club serving over 600 diners daily. Meanwhile, the grill overflows with cuts and entrails at barrio favourite *Parrilla Peña* (Centro). The go-to order never fails: a "bife de chorizo" (sirloin), fries, and a bottle of Malbec. On a picturesque corner of San Telmo, bodegón *Gran Parrilla del* *Plata*'s white-shirted waiters bring old-school porteño charm at a reasonable price. *Nuestra Parrilla* (pictured) is a casual hole in the wall inside San Telmo market, where Freddy cooks a supreme "choripán". Snagging a table at upscale *Don Julio* (Palermo) is a challenge. But one taste of its juicy grass-fed steak, seasoned only with salt, will justify Argentina's beef reputation.
• Various locations, see Index p.60

After initiating MALBA's collection of contemporary Argentine art during her time as curator, Inés was recruited to inaugurate and direct the art department at Torcuato Di Tella University. She's published extensively on contemporary art, produced high-profile shows across the city, and curated the Argentine Pavilion at the 52nd Venice Biennale

Inés Katzenstein, Curator

Aesthetic View

Inés Katzenstein knows art—and the Buenos Aires art scene knows her too. She weaves us into the humming world of artist-run spaces, as well as revealing some secret gardens to erase the concrete feeling, the wild overgrown debris wilderness on the edge of the city and places to suitably mark Argentina's troubled past

"Micro-political concepts from daily life" are probed by Argentine and Latin American artists within Hache Galeria

You helped create the Art Department at Torcuato di Tella University, can you tell us a little about your job there?
My role is to direct our main programme—the Artists' Programme—it's extracurricular, for artists and curators. We get about 20 artists and six curators a year. I decide what we teach, the professors, the structure. We've also got a film department and we put on a series of exhibitions. About 300 people apply per year—it's a very intense programme with a practical, experimental and theoretical aspect to it.

Where do you take friends when they're visiting?
I take them to see art shows and out to eat. *Miramar* is a Spanish restaurant, kind of like our "bodegones", but this one seems straight out of a tiny town in Spain. The food is delicious, very

traditional. As if the world of cool things never passed by. But I recently had my best meal ever at *La Mar*. It's a Peruvian cevichería in Palermo. It's incredible.

Are there any emerging artists you'd recommend us to keep an eye out for?
There are way too many artists to list here, but if I had to name a couple I'd say Eduardo Navarro and Sol Pipkin. They're in their mid-30s. Eduardo works with eccentric projects, open formats and specific themes to do with nature, animality, religion—he changes the form of his work even though his interests are very clear. He's eccentric, unpredictable—I like that.

Where do you have your most satisfying shopping sprees?
For clothing, I love *Chicco Ruiz – DAM* and *Dubié*. DAM is very

A secluded garden is the setting for cocktails, music nights—or just breakfast—at Palermo Hollywood's boutique hotel Home

baroque and artisanal. They might make one of every piece, and they work a lot with collage, which I think is great. Dubié is the exact opposite—very minimalistic clothing. Then I love to go book shopping, especially at *La Internacional Argentina* and *Librería Punc*. They're not mainstream at all, they're very special. La Internacional belongs to an art and architecture publisher called Mansalva. The bookstore stocks literature and has new and used books—it's a meeting point for local artists and friends. There are book presentations and readings. And Punc is a tiny comics store. It's incredibly small, but has the most amazing comic books you can imagine—Argentine and international. They're both in Villa Crespo, a neighbourhood starting to enjoy some cultural movement, which is fantastic.

What about the city's hidden secrets?

I'd recommend a hunt for gardens. Buenos Aires is kind of ugly and grey. So I think it's a good idea to propose handsome, green spaces—otherwise you're always trapped in the cement. It's not like London or New York where there are always green spaces waiting for you, it feels like these places are little secrets in Buenos Aires. *Home Hotel* has a beautiful garden. I love to have meetings there and eat breakfast in the garden. I also love the garden of the *Museo de Arte Español Enrique Larreta*. The museum itself is utterly uninteresting—it houses antique Spanish art—but it has the best garden in Buenos Aires. It's perfect to walk and chat with friends. Maybe it's not great for a drink but it's definitely somewhere to meet girl-friends when they need to talk to me about their issues. A place few people know about is the *Museo Xul Solar*, the house of the man of the same name. Inventor, mystic, painter... an artist like no other.

Where else for outdoor inspiration?

The *Reserva Ecológica Costanera Sur* and *Reserva Ecológica Vicente López*. Both of these nature reserves are on the river. The Costanera Sur one is an enormous space on the water that was filled in and the vegetation has run wild. These days it's pretty civilised but it was a darker place in the 1980-90s—a gay cruising area. There's a horrendous debris beach from all the landfill, which pops out from beneath it towards the coast. It's a totally bizarre landscape and I love it. Then there's the *Parque de la Memoria*, a memorial to the people who disappeared during the last Argentine dictatorship. It's also on the coast and honestly a fantastic place. It's also a very impressive place geographically, with intensely emotional architecture. It's a nice place to have a picnic. The dictatorship, for those who don't know, was from 1976 and 1983; it was a military dictatorship with state-led terrorism of horrifying dimensions—30,000 people disappeared. The most famous result are the Madres de la Plaza de Mayo, a group of mothers who took on the junta to search for their children, opening a legal process that's still ongoing. To this day, every year there are still grandchildren whose true identity is discovered. There are various landmarks—another is Plaza de Mayo, with Thursday marches in front of the Casa Rosada. Another is *ESMA*, the former military mechanic's school, which became a torture centre. It was turned into a museum with very good shows.

Architecturally, what are your tips?

Definitely the Edificio Kavanagh and anything by Clorindo Testa. He was a fantastic brutalist architect from the 1970s, and his greatest example is the *Biblioteca Nacional* (national library). It's a concrete UFO. It even looks unfinished—futuristic but dystopic. It's fantastic. Also *La Casa de la Cultura*. It was the house of the writer Victoria Ocampo, designed by Alejandro Bustillo.

What can you tell us about the young arts scene in Buenos Aires?

There's a growing arts scene of artist-run spaces—they don't last long, but mobilise a very interesting set of young people. There's *Hache*, *Mite*, *Formosa* and *UV*. They've all got very different profiles. Mite and Hache are more traditional in that they have gallerists, a list of artists— they're a little more formal. UV is the craziest, it focusses more on performance and things like gender issues. Formosa is more like a shop where they give needlepoint lessons—it leans more towards crafts. There's a huge scene, it's very effervescent. Plenty of interested people without much money... There are few collectionists, but tons of artists—a lot of energy.

What would you change in the city?

The city is a total mess—there are too many cars, you can't circulate. It's changing a lot, but it's becoming more chaotic, with more social inequality, creating a ton of problems—paranoia, confrontation, aggression. I'd like to see all that change. It's a complicated city and it's getting more so. Poorer and poorer, more social conflict and a reduction in politicians' ability to face reality. They don't want to recognise it. They're always directing their messages to this imaginary middle-class neighbour who almost doesn't exist anymore. Lucky for us we've got an enormous ability to adapt, but things like the public transport system just don't work.

Wander through the quiet barrio of Colegiales to find ample art both on the streets—and in the eclectic Formosa Galería

Villa Crespo & Almagro
Soul of the City

Geographically central to the capital, these neighbourhoods have a traditional, residential vibe, threaded through with tango haunts, closed-door bars and art galleries sprouting along tree-lined streets

Culture **Space Invaders**

Residential barrio Villa Crespo long kept a low profile next to rampantly gentrified Palermo. But in recent years it's become something of an art hub. Respected gallery *Ruth Benzacar* was one of the pioneers, moving from its downtown space in order to satisfy the greater spatial needs of today's contemporary art. Another key stop on the new circuit is *Slyzmud*, whose "Sala 2" (pictured) hosts active and arresting installations by mostly Argentine artists. Also showcasing Argentine creators is *Nora Fisch*, especially those dealing in bold conceptual work. Along with other spaces like *Gachi Prieto*—focussed on Latin American art—and *La Ira de Dios*—which provides residences and cultural events—you're sure to find enough artistic stimulation under the leafy branches of the barrio's charming roads.
• Villa Crespo, various locations, see Index p.60

Outdoors Central Park

At the capital's centre lies *Parque Centenario*. Though technically in the barrio of Caballito, it's sandwiched between Villa Crespo and Almagro and makes up a central part of local life. You'll see joggers in lycra circling the circular park, along with families sipping mate, friends having a smoke, and a lake teeming with koi carp and swans. An amphitheatre hosts outdoor shows and markets crop up during the week. On weekends it explodes, with a crafts fair, book stalls and live bands. Within the park is the *Museo Argentino de Ciencias Naturales* and an astronomical observatory offering occasional free viewings.
• Caballito, various locations, see Index p.60

Food   Mama's Kitchen

Parrilla, pizza, and pasta: three Ps that pretty much sum up Italo-Argentine cuisine. And that's what you get at *La Mamma Rosa*, a lost-in-time neighbourhood cantina where portions are large and prices are cheap. Here, there's something for the entire family—whether a steak off the grill, creamy homemade pasta, thick-crust pizza, or "milanesa napolitana a caballo"—a schnitzel topped with tomato sauce, ham, cheese, and a fried egg, with a side of mashed potatoes. Despite its local no-frills charm, reserving is a must... Just brush up on your Spanish first, because you're unlikely to find English spoken.
• La Mamma Rosa, Jufré 202, Villa Crespo

Food   Sea Fruits

Even the meatiest of meat eaters need a break. And *I Latina*, a reservation-only "puerta cerrada" (closed-door restaurant), in a beautiful restored house in Villa Crespo's "leather district", provides a gastronomic trip to Colombia's beaches. The Macías siblings offer Caribbean and tropical flavours: think a seven-course tasting menu with dishes like smoked shrimp, sole, and caramelised octopus ceviche, fresh fish with coconut and anise, and sugar cane and coffee-glazed pork shoulder. The menu is paired with top boutique Argentine wines.
• I Latina, Murillo 725, Villa Crespo, ilatinabuenosaires.com

Home Again

Years after establishing herself as one of the local fashion scene's most fearless creators, Jessica Trosman came full circle—and set up shop in the same place she'd sewed her first pieces. These days, the showroom looks nothing like her father's mechanic shop, though the humble surroundings remain mostly unchanged. Here, opposite Atlanta football stadium and far from Palermo's shiny boutiques, Trosman displays the timeless, monochrome pieces from her *JT* line. Pop into adjoining café *Yeite* for a coffee or pastry, ideally to see the Atlanta faithful file out.
• JT & Yeite, Humboldt 291-293, Villa Crespo, trosman.com.ar

Food   Defining Factura

Argentines eat late—starting at 9pm—so "merienda" is the much needed afternoon snack. It's also the time when friends gather to chat and gossip over mate or coffee, and "facturas". These very Argentine pastries were introduced long ago by Italian anarchist bakers and have anti-clerical names as a result. Try the "cañoncito con dulce de leche" and other treats at *Las Violetas*, an iconic café with marble floors and stained-glass windows dating back to 1884. The way to go is the María Cala, a silver platter piled with tasty cakes, sandwiches, and facturas—a pleno.
• Las Violetas, Avenida Rivadavia 3899, Almagro, lasvioletas.com

Night   Knock It

The beautiful doors of Buenos Aires—just try not to photograph at least one—conceal all manner of pleasures. Bars, for example. Sometimes to avoid taxes, other times to create a reputation. Villa Crespo's *878* (pictured) was one of the first—the door reveals a massive speakeasy with creative cocktails, dining options and even a dancefloor. Less famed, and with a more bohemian vibe, is *Ladran Sancho* (Almagro). The patio is the heart of the place, and there's a little stage where a jam takes place on Tuesdays, alongside other creative antics.
• 878, Thames 878, Villa Crespo, 878bar.com.ar; Ladran Sancho, Guardia Vieja 3811, Almagro

Food · Night   Patrimonial Pasta

The barrio of Almagro is known for its tango credentials, with classic spots like *El Boliche de Roberto* for drinking ginebra with ancient, pickled singers, *La Catedral*, the milonga inside a kooky mansion—and many more. But the tango encyclopedia names its oldest standing landmark as *Pierino* (pictured). Opened by Calabrian owners in 1909, the legacy has stayed in the family ever since. And the restaurant has been a long-time hangout for famous musicians, including the likes of Astor Piazzolla, Enrique Cadícamo, Aníbal Troilo, Julián Centeya and Charly García. But though it's designated as a cultural landmark, it should also be recommended as a culinary one.

The specialty here is the homemade pasta. Though it might be hard to choose from the seemingly infinite menu, unchanged in decades, you can't fail with Patagonian lamb ravioli, fusilli al fierrito, or eggplant parmesan. In good Argentine tradition, turn up on the 29th day of every month to dine on "ñoquis" (gnocchi). And be sure to sample the tiramisu—after all, according to the owner it's "the best in the world." For a pre-pasta Italian aperitif like Cinzano with soda and lemon, or a post-prandial digestif like Fernet, the old school *Café El Banderín* is just a few blocks away.

• Almagro, various locations, see Index Index p.60

Ingrid Beck & Mariano Lucano, Journalist & Illustrator

Critical Thinking

Founders of legendary Buenos Aires satirical magazine "Revista Barcelona", Ingrid and Mariano have been in a fair share of confrontation with the establishment since they started their fearless mission of mockery in 2004. Ingrid also presents an influential show on national radio and is the founder of the journalism school Tea-Arte, while Mariano has made his name as a leading graphic artist and illustrator

A city forged from immigration on the periphery of empire has created a fascinating local personality. The origin of the porteños' unique and razor sharp wit is explored by the city's crack satirists. They also reveal the best way to find out what Peronism even means, and some essential reading to get into a Buenos Aires state of mind

How would you define porteño humour, and where does it come from?

Mariano: It's extremely acidic, extremely corrosive, and of course there's always a victim. Buenos Aires has had a lot of DNA, fruit of centuries of immigration. Another factor has been its situation on the periphery—it was never in the economic or geographic centre of the world—this also created a particular local character.

What do you like most and least about the city?

Ingrid: I like that it's a big city with a lot of alternatives—even if I don't do them, I like that they are there. I like all the restaurants and the bars... What I don't like is the disorganised transport, and the bad mood of the porteños.

Mariano: For me the city is the best because it has a lot of people and activity. And what I like least is that the economic situation always means an uphill struggle. This can be an advantage because it acts as a stimulus, but you also have to do more to produce anything.

How would you like it to change?

Ingrid: It's an impossible wish, but I'd love a beach. There's a huge coast that is not taken advantage of, with contaminated water. If you cross the river to Montevideo or even Colonia de Uruguay, they take advantage of the coast, but we don't. I'd love to be able to put up a parasol.

What's your home area like?

Mariano: I live in the barrio of Monserrat, on the border with San Telmo. The city was founded 500 years ago in these neighbourhoods. I like that it's still a barrio—beyond the influence of tourism. There are "almacenes" (groceries), not just supermarkets. And there's local activity, people drinking mate in the street, that kind of thing. Yet we're still ten blocks from the centre so it's well connected, while retaining its local idiosyncrasy.

Ingrid: I live in Colegiales, which I like a lot. I live in a "PH" (old-style house), with a patio and terrace with parrilla. It's a middle-class neighbourhood that still conserves its local feeling. In my block I have trees on the street, and an old-school grocer, a kind of shop that's vanishing. They greet me like a neighbour. People still wash their cars on the pavement... And there's no high rises—on my block at least.

Where do you like to eat?

Mariano: In my area, there's a lot of food from around the world and around Argentina. One to recommend is *Jhabibi*, a Middle Eastern restaurant. I love their shawarma. I'd also recommend *La Carretería*, which serves empanadas salteñas (Salta-style), like with "carne cortada al cuchillo" (beef chunks). Argentines eat a lot of empanadas. There's also a well known parrilla called *El Chiquilín de Bachín*. They even have tango there. It's expensive, but you eat very well.

Argentine pizza is quite sensational. Where's the best?

Ingrid: *Güerrín* is one of the best, but *Angelín* is also very good.

Mariano: Yes, Güerrín is the best—I go there a lot. One block away is *Banchero*, where they invented pizza with onion. Well they say they did, anyway. Opposite there you have *Los Inmortales*: it's expensive but it has an aura. Supposedly Carlos Gardel ate there.

What about the best milanesa?

Mariano: There's one place called *El Palacio de la Papa Frita* that honours the dish pretty well. They marry the fries with the milanesa in an incredible way.

Where do you go for drinks after work?

Ingrid: For a beer in the evening, *Los Galgos* is great—a classic right in the centre. It was closed a long time and then a young restaurateur reopened it. He bought all the original pieces of décor, rebuilt it, and now it's very lovely. Otherwise, to have cocktails and eat good food there's *Bar 878*.

The city does cafés extremely well. Any favourites?

Mariano: Our office is pretty close to *Café La Paz*, legendary because all the intellectuals in the 1960s and 1970s came through there. I also like *Celta Bar*, which is classified as a "bar notable"—one of the magnificent, century-old cafés of Buenos Aires.

How can visitors get acquainted with the culture of the city?

Mariano: They should go to *Museo Evita*. It was originally a residence for single mothers until the family of Eva Perón took it over. They put all her clothes there and photos from the time; and they tell the whole story of what Peronism was, until her death in 1952.

Ingrid: It's great because we always try to explain to foreigners what Peronism is—it's very difficult. At least at Museo Evita they can see some of the relics.

Any other museums?

Ingrid: The *Malba*. I love the design of the museum itself, the permanent collection is excellent—it has fascinating Latin American artists, and the special exhibitions are very good. The shop is beautiful, and the surrounding area too.

Mariano: The *Museo Nacional de Bellas Artes* is a museum that, beyond its Argentine art, has a small but excellent collection of Renaissance art. It's great because they have one painting from each of the important guys. Check out the room of Baroque Spanish art. Another, which flies under the radar, is *Fundación Klemm*. It's a private museum with free entry, and has a 20th-century collection that's pretty complete. They also have one work from each artist. And as the 20th century is lacking at Bellas Artes, Klemm rounds off your experience.

Ingrid: Another nice one is the *Museo de Ciencias Naturales*, inside Parque Centenario. It has dinosaurs—it's great to go with kids.

How can visitors best get to know the city?

Ingrid: I think you have to walk —that's the best way. The centre, Sunday in San Telmo, Thursday night in Palermo, Recoleta... There are beautiful places to go walking, and slowly you'll contaminate yourself with Buenos Aires.

Mariano: Definitely walking through San Telmo, which is amazing... There might not be any 500-year-old houses left, but some architectural fragments and even whole streets are 200 years old. The streets of Balcarce and Defensa are beautiful. I also love Chile, blocks 200-800—it's very pretty, and there's also a lot of good restaurants. In particular, try *Café San Juan la Cantina*, and I'd also recommend *Garage Bar San Telmo*. It's not well known, but it's huge. They have old gas stoves and a couple of old cars—it's like some kind of garage for racecars. It's very chilled.

Talking of food, where else is good?

Ingrid: I love a cantina called *Los Amigos*. It's good for eating with a group of friends—it's very cheap and very tasty—but the idea is they serve you whatever they've made that day. Their "flan" with dulce de leche is more like dulce de leche with flan. *Amorinda* for me has pretty much the best pasta in the world. It

The legendary downtown pizzería Güerrín has kept its wood-burning oven going constantly since it opened in 1932

belongs to a family from Mar de las Pampas. The homemade pasta is amazing and the "berenjena en escabeche" (marinated aubergine) is the best on the planet. And the best sushi is at *M*.

Do you ever go to listen to music?
    Ingrid: There's the *Club Atlético Fernandez Fierro*, a very special kind of regular tango concert. Then, there's jazz club *Notorious*, and *Bebop Club* is worth checking out.

How do you escape from the dirty world of politics?
    Ingrid: I learn singing, and I also do boxing... Those are my escapes. And eating out with friends, always.
    Mariano: I love art, and luckily Buenos Aires has a lot going on. Right now for example, there's one on Picasso drawings, a show of the Russian artist Malevich, and an

exhibition of little known drawings by Berni, probably our finest artist.

What book would you recommend someone visiting for the first time?
    Ingrid: There's a very beautiful book, "Una Muchacha Muy Bella" by Julián López. Also, check out the writer Selva Almada, whose books are very Argentine—not porteño, but Argentine—both in the stories themselves and how she tells them.
    Mariano: Though Jorge Luis Borges died more than 30 years ago, he remains unavoidable when it comes to thinking about Buenos Aires. Fundamentally because he has a universal language. He manages to universalise the city, treating it as if it were Babylon, without blurring the outlines of what Buenos Aires is.

Crackling Asphalt

Josefina Licitra

When my neighbour moved away she left her bicycle with me for a few days. She said she didn't have the strength to cycle to her new house after so many hours of moving. I didn't understand why she didn't put it in the van with her furniture, but I didn't let this bother me. I stashed it in my patio. The bike was heavy, the brakes were stiff and there were spider webs in the spokes. But still, I looked at it longingly. I'd been wanting to cycle again for a while.

Two weeks later I got it fixed and started using it. Three weeks later, expecting my neighbour to come back and get it—something that never happened—I bought a bike for myself. That's how it all began. I don't have a car and wanted to move around without going through the procedures, tests and expenses involved in being a driver. Or at least that was my thinking at first. What I didn't have in mind was the other part. That apart from being an accessible form of transport, the bicycle is a point of view from which you can construct a perspective both intimate and urban. Architecture, relations between people, the ways in which we are accompanied or alone, the demolitions, buildings and advertising billboards that alter the porteño fabric: all of this changes. A few centimetres above the ground Buenos Aires, fourteenth most bikeable city in the world—according to "Wired", which gives it first spot in Latin America—is a different capital city to the one I've known during forty years of living here.

The Monday I got my first bike—I now have two—I debuted it by night in Bajo Flores, an area in the west of the city. On Carabobo Avenue at the 1500 block, near the shanty town Villa 1-11-14, there's a hub of wonderful and cheap Korean restaurants run by the community living around there. Maybe it was the alcohol or the tiredness, or the cobbled street—or an anxiety in my cycling because Bajo Flores, around midnight, is not a good place to be ambling about. But what is certain is I took a curb at a 30-degree angle, lost my balance and ended up on the floor, bleeding.

"Boludaaaa!" shouted Alejandro—who's now my partner. It was our first outing and I, with a few beers to my name, wanted to impress him with a fancy manoeuvre. The result was an accident, some blood, a hug, a first kiss.

Since then, one year later, my knee has a kind of supernova of dark sparkles. The scar is, in its way, beautiful. I look at it—touch it—when I want to remember the origin of so many good things.

Not long after this fall I started my love affair, as well, with the place in which I live. Buenos Aires is different when you see it at 20 kilometres per hour, without any windows in between. On the bike, your sphere is the street. It is so in the pedestrian's world too, but the wheels allow a perfect transience: you can mentally sketch what you see, and at the same time let everything go, because the city always keeps on. In that sense, cycling is a bit like journalism.

The bicycle is, in fact, a point of view. A few centimetres above the ground and with movement as the main guarantee of stability—if you don't keep advancing, you fall—Buenos Aires breaks its own armour and shows a lovelier body—one that is more alive, even. The city has 150 kilometres of safe transit—the cycle paths—and in some barrios, like Palermo, San Telmo and Barrio Norte, there's a kind of fraternity of people welcoming to cyclists. There are "bike-friendly" bars and restaurants, where they lend you locks and pumps and even offer discounts if you come by bike. And there are car parks that don't charge you.

I tend to use them. In Buenos Aires it's a good idea to put away your bike every time you're going in somewhere for a long time and you won't be able to check the street. Though there are strong locks, the universe of the porteño cyclist is overflowing with stories of vehicles abducted, sci-fi-movie style. That's why car parks, if there's one nearby, are the best option. Because sometimes—as mentioned—they don't even charge you. And because even if they do, the price is negligible: ten percent of the price for a car, some 50 cents per hour.

Every time I pay very little—or nothing at all—I feel free. Every time I see people shut up in their cars, barely poking an elbow out a lowered window, I feel free. Every time I zig zag between cars stuck in long, ugly jams, I feel free. And every time it rains, as well, I feel free. I found this out a few days after buying my first bicycle, when in the middle of the street I was hit by a downpour. I had to be wary of the brakes and potential skidding on corners, but aside from that the experience was almost hallucinogenic: the trees shone, the asphalt crackled like a record. I went up and down the empty avenues—it's not true that Buenos Aires is flat—I felt my muscles burning beneath the water, and then I understood that the city is a form of nature. I suppose that's one of the virtues of animal-powered transport: the effort, alternating with letting yourself flow down the slopes, produces a specific per- spective, vaguely enlightened, which helps you take ownership of an urban space that's normally hostile.

The day of that rainfall I arrived home, sat in front of the laptop and wrote a short text that I then uploaded to the social networks. Minutes after posting, a mail arrived. It was from a peer who'd just read it, who edits a cycling magazine and wanted to interview me as an amateur urban cyclist. I accepted, knowing I didn't have anything relevant to say. The most intimate thing I shared during the interview was my first bicycle-related memory. I must have been eight, I was cycling on the pavement and I saw that a few metres ahead there was a whole family blocking the way. As I didn't have a horn, I started to shout "excuse me, pee, pee, pee"—but nobody heard. And for some reason I discarded the option of braking. I had to decide which of the family I would hit. I hit the dad.

—Bicycles connect with childhood—said my interviewer.

I said yes: a connection to childhood is another reason why we choose to cycle. But that's the rational explanation. The other, as always, is in the shadows.

It's two in the morning. I had dinner with Alejandro in Palermo— where most of the restaurants are—and we cycled back to his place, in Zona Norte, the northern part of the Buenos Aires metropolitan area. In a few days it will be a year since our first outing in Bajo Flores. The scar remains on my knee. But the rest of it all has evolved, including my relationship with the bicycle. I'm good at cycling. With the passage of time I ended up believing that the city, when I'm on two wheels, belongs to me completely. The feeling becomes sharper at night. Then, Buenos Aires is a wasteland and I take full advantage. I ride with my arms folded, zig zag, ride with my eyes closed, ride along holding hands with my man. I imagine I'm the Esther Williams of bicycles. Every so often

I see some porter smoking in a doorway and we look at each other with a knowing calmness, as if we were both intruders in the same empty house.

All the rest is mute, and night.

Once we arrived in Zona Norte, we decided to keep cycling on to the river. Vicente López, Olivos, La Lucila and San Isidro are part of a beautiful coastal route that connects with the Río de la Plata and on which, any day of the week, it's easy to do everything that's difficult in the city: to ride while looking at the horizon, amid a safe environment—the whole area has quiet streets and bicycle routes for happy circulation—and to deposit the wheels a few metres away, without locking up, in order to sit down and contemplate the water, free from the worry that somebody will pass by and steal it.

To get there, so as not to cycle too far, there's the Tigre branch of the Mitre train—it starts in Retiro station, but there are stations in the middle like Belgrano—with the first and last carriages dedicated to bikes. From Vicente López station there are then three hectares of ecological reserve to roam—the bike left out of it—with a vista of swamps, a gallery forest, birds and lizards roaming free.

But the most beautiful part of the landscape is the river. And the night. Now, sitting on the grass, I see in the distance, in a remote crook of the coast, the accumulation of porteño lights that lean together like sociable lunatics in a psychiatric commune. With perspective, Buenos Aires seems a little boisterous and hostile. But at the same time it looks small: possible. And it allows a rewriting of Junichiro Tanizaki's idea in his book "In Praise of Shadows": if it's true—as Tanizaki says— that nobody should live in a house they can't clean by themselves, then maybe nobody should live in a city they can't explore on their own.

Josefina Licitra, born in 1975, is an award-winning Argentine journalist, editor and narrator. Publications she writes for include "Piauí" (Brazil), "Letras Libres" (Mexico) and "Internazionale" (Italy). She has published several books including "Los Otros. Una historia del conurbano bonarense" ("The Others. A history of the Buenos Aires metropolitan area")

Tasteful Tale

One of the biggest Argentine names in gastronomy, Fernando cut his teeth under celebrity chef Francis Mallmann. A love for honest, simple food is a recurring theme in his projects—from one of Buenos Aires' hottest restaurants to his beachside kitchen in Uruguay, European endeavours with restaurant chain Los Gauchos and a slew of TV shows

Though his work sees him travelling on a regular basis, Fernando is a Buenos Aires man through and through. Classic cafés, specials cuts of meat and hot new eateries are some of what he shares when asked about his beloved city

What are you working on right now?

I'm putting everything together for the high season in Uruguay, assembling the team for the kitchen, the bakers, setting the opening date and organising events with the chefs who will be visiting Santa Teresita. I'm also going to London next week to organise "Diez Manos" —an event we've been hosting for years where four colleagues and I prepare a meal together.

What's your relationship to Buenos Aires?

I'm porteño—I was born here, raised here. I choose to live here. I've lived abroad during certain times of my life, but this is still the city I choose to live in. I love this city, I find it an interesting place to live. It's the city I know the most.

Which areas do you move around in the most?

For years it's been Zona Norte. I live in La Lucila, close to Vicente López and my restaurant, *Sucre*, is very close by. I try to keep my affairs to this part of the city. Zona Norte is a very quiet area, filled with houses and lots of green—very far removed from the bustle and the insanity of the city centre, from which I try to escape as much as I can. It's got a really tranquil, almost town-like feel to it, with a little shopping strip with everything you need for the house. You can ride around on your bicycle, there's less pollution, fewer cars. It's wonderful.

What's the quintessential Buenos Aires dish?

"Milanesa a la napolitana"—a true Argentinism. It's a deformation of the milanesa (breaded steak) made by Argentineans. Another one is "matambre" (rolled cured meat) with Russian salad, or tongue in vinaigrette. These are all classic "bodegón" (tavern) dishes—my association for classic porteño food.

I don't really eat milanesas a la napolitana anymore, I think I'd have to spend a month in bed to recover from that. But I know they do them especially well in places like *Los Galgos*, a classic old café that's been around since 1930. They recently restored it beautifully, keeping the old look of the place, and now they just serve classic Buenos Aires food.

Where else for some authentic Argentine flavour in town?

It's not specifically Argentine, but Buenos Aires has a historic connection to Italy. I like to go every now and then to *Il Matterello*, a very good Italian restaurant in La Boca. It's a family-run place that's been around forever, and I like to go there for basically everything. It's all good there, they're Italian! There's also *Don Julio*, another lifelong parrilla, where I like to go and take people. They do a great "ojo de bife" (rib eye), which isn't on the menu.

Where to go for creative cooking?

Germán Martitegui is doing really great work with his restaurant *Tegui*, besides his other projects. *Proper* is a restaurant that's been set up in a former auto repair shop in Palermo. They've got two chefs and a pastry chef working in an open kitchen with a big brick oven. They do small plates that change with the seasons or according to what they can find—the food is quite simple but super well done. It's not a pretentious restaurant at all and I think they're hitting it out of the park. *Gran Dabbang* is another small restaurant run by a chef named Mariano Ramón; he's young and he's got a great track record. He and his wife set up the restaurant; their food is heavily influenced by Indian flavours but they take interesting liberties with it. I think it's one of the better developments in town from the last few years.

Mishiguene
Palermo

Hong Kong Style
Belgrano

If you had time to escape Buenos Aires for a day, where'd you go?

To Córdoba. I love the hills, the landscape. Cordobés asparagus is, by the way, very delicious right now.

We can't have all this without a glass of wine—what's your tip?

Well, I could talk about wine all day long, but even though I love wine and I love to drink it, I'm not an oenologist. I'm still learning. We've got great wines here in Argentina. For a long time, Mendoza was the cradle of Argentine wine, but now you have vineyards in Salta, Patagonia, La Rioja—there's tons of great new wines and many talented young oenologists doing interesting things. I'd say to venture outside of the classic Malbec. There's no doubt we have excellent Malbec, but I wouldn't reduce Argentine wine to just that grape. The Alma Negra vineyard does excellent wine; Ernesto Catena is doing a great job with that. I'd also recommend anything from Piedra Infinita.

How does Buenos Aires influence you in your work as a chef?

So many ways, but then again everything is a constant influence. I am always moved by the things I see on the street, things I hear, people.

Are any food markets good for the travelling shopper?

Whichever one's closest to them. People have to go back to the neighbourhood fruit and vegetable stand. Besides the weekly farmers' markets that pop up in every area, we need to visit our local produce man. We need it so that those places can survive and start improving quality again.

Could you describe each neighbourhood using a different kind of food?

La Boca would be Italian food, San Telmo would be coffee—at any of the cafés sitting on Plaza Dorrego. Palermo would be modern cooking. El Once would be Jewish food—though there's a really good new place called *Mishiguene* in Palermo. Flores would be Korean food and Chinatown obviously Chinese. My favourite there is *Hong Kong Style*, it's a classic. And parrilla, of course, would be the whole city.

You spend a lot of time abroad—what could London learn from Buenos Aires?

If they could catch a little of our climate that would be amazing. They could do with being a little more informal, as well. I think Argentina—Latin America in general, actually—is great at human contact. Passing on a little of our warmth would not be bad at all.

What would you like to see change in the city?

The political class. Hopefully it will start changing. But that's not what we're here to discuss. I'd love to see changes in professionalism, the work ethic. It would be great to recover the work ethic that existed in Argentina during my grandparents' time. I feel that's been lost.

Are the porteños adventurous eaters?

They used not to be, but with time it's really changing. They're much more adventurous than a few years ago. I think as long as new projects and places are presented and this culture of travel persists, it'll continue this way.

In an old auto repair shop, the chefs at Proper cook up seasonal treats in a big brick oven

True cocktail culture is relatively new to the city, anywhere for an interesting nightcap?

Florería Atlántico does fantastic cocktails, their whole menu is good. Los Galgos that I mentioned already for food, is also a good place for drinks, as is the speakeasy-like *Frank's* in Palermo.

How do you feel about Buenos Aires' future?

Very optimistic, actually. I think that as long as the state allows it, the gastronomy scene has a lot of ground to cover, lots to develop, lots to show.

Where have you been going to eat since you were a kid?

Happening—it's a traditional Buenos Aires parrilla that's been around for about 50 years. I still go, and I still love it.

Speaking of Italian influences, Buenos Aires loves ice cream. Where can we go for a really good scoop?

Definitely *Heladería Scannapieco* —it's a traditional ice-cream shop managed by an Italian family.

What makes an empanada good? Where can we get it in Buenos Aires?

The best empanadas are the ones you make at home. For an empanada to be good it has to be made with fresh ingredients, good dough and, very importantly, baked well. The best empanadas are from the provinces of Salta and Mendoza.

Are there any classy cafés perfect for some authentic neighbourhood vibes?

Café Tortoni is a great place to have a coffee and settle in for a chat with friends.

Latam Glam

A showcase by Marcos López

The self-proclaimed "Andy Warhol of the underdeveloped" presents a world of drama, humour and saturated hues. What follows is a selection from "Pop Latino", a series that's taken the artist on the road in search of the cultural idiosyncrasies that divide and unite his land

An award-winning designer
with roots in theatre and
graphics, Martín's avant-garde
brand Tramando focusses on
textile experimentation and
has made him almost as
beloved in Tokyo as he is in his
hometown of Buenos Aires

Martín Churba, Fashion Designer

Dream Weaver

In a rare melding of the two qualities, Martín is both a dreamer and
a doer. His creations have always come from the heart, made with
the thinking woman in mind. Here, the visionary designer lets us in
on his city, as seen from Libertador Avenue

What's your relationship with Buenos Aires?

It's always been my city—I've never left it for more than four months. It's funny, I've lived and worked all along Libertador Avenue, which stretches across the whole capital. It's like I've been moving on one axis. Libertador is so beautiful, because it goes through all Palermo's parks—it's the principal artery connecting the city to the river. Being close to Libertador means being close to the water. I live two blocks from the Río de la Plata, just outside the city in Martínez. You can see the river from my doorstep. My relationship to the city is pretty diverse; there's an entire social aspect that makes it so Latin American. I think there are two Buenos Aires: there's a much poorer Buenos Aires than the one along Libertador Avenue— I've developed a relationship to that Buenos Aires as well, neighbourhoods like La Matanza, La Juanita. In 2004 with the Guardapolvos project I visited La Juanita and began to understand these contradictions we live with in the same city, making us such an unhappy society. I've been working for the past few years towards this integration—of course from a design point of view. The desire to connect, reach and relate to that other Buenos Aires and that other reality.

You've always operated on the fringes of fashion—is the porteña open to experimentation?

In that context, the porteña lives with a double-edged knife. On the one hand, she's got style and class, by which I mean she achieves great results through finding a fashion identity. But on the other hand, she's a victim of that class and that style—she's practically corseted into a cliché. There's an original idea, classy and stylish, but at the same time she sells herself short because it's just repetition—there's no true aesthetic liberty. There's an enormous aesthetic agenda here, related to hair salons, manicures, waxing, cosmetics, nutrition, and on top of that, fashion. It's a tyrannical combo for women, which doesn't connect to their potential; rather, it limits them to a very specific model.

How do you see Buenos Aires' fashion in ten years?

Buenos Aires could be evolving towards being a capital that values and looks after its entrepreneurs and creators, stimulating new projects and looking after existing ones because of a local identity, and thanks to the history of local fashion. Or it will prioritise international fashion, which seeks only to sell a model replicated a million times in some other place, and whose only goal in markets like these is to expand its sales a little. I think it would obviously be better for our society if we made sure to guard the projects that speak to our identity, while accepting that it doesn't depend on one player, rather a collective.

Tell us about the neighbourhood you work in.

Tramando's neighbourhood is a beautiful area. It has that central porteño feel, close to the parks and the old architecture of the city. But at the same time it relates to a contemporary vision of a Latin American city, and to descendants of European immigrants. Coming to our flagship store Tramando is a wonderful experience, pretty much what you'd choose as a walk through the city. It's the Buenos Aires sidewalks with that wonderful mix of Latin and Parisian, very current but filled with old architecture. The neighbourhood also offers the *Cementerio de la Recoleta*, a beautiful place to walk through and

Left is "Manifestación" ("Demonstration", 1934) by Antonio Berni, one of many key Latin American works at MALBA

again, filled with contrasts—you've got Evita's grave and other characters from Buenos Aires' history. There are upscale dining options like *Sottovoce* and *Fervor*—high-quality places where the food is next level.

Where should we go to understand Argentine design?

The parks and museums, especially those in Recoleta that are part of this cultural mix. I'm thinking of the area that reaches *MALBA*, passes the *Museo Nacional de Arte Decorativo*, the *Museo Nacional de Bellas Artes* and the *Museo de Arquitectura y Diseño (MARQ)*. We're surrounded by very emblematic buildings, four blocks away from Nueve de Julio Avenue. You can walk through the whole area and feel you've got Buenos Aires in the palm of your hand.

You've worked in cities like Tokyo— what could it learn from Buenos Aires?

This idea of what different cities could trade with each other is very interesting. Tokyo is one of the most different places from anywhere else I've known, especially because of its climate of silence. That might be one of my favourite things in any city. Buenos Aires has, in turn, its own texture, a certain vibration, its own perfume—these things reach into places that are extremely powerful. Many people come from Japan and are deeply moved by this city. On the other hand, the fact we sit at the end of an enormous continent with such a beautiful climate, I think somehow translates into wonderful people. Gestures, ways of moving, souls—something special in a faraway place.

When your friends come to visit, where do you take them?

They have to see Buenos Aires' most urban face—the old centre, San Telmo. During the day, night, weekdays, weekends. That's where the history of Buenos Aires lives. And, of course, beautiful places like the parks—Palermo, the *Bosques de Palermo*. Libertador Avenue is fantastic. I also like the river, I love the Costanera Sur, Costanera Norte. I like all of Zona Norte as well as Tigre. And I'm especially fond of the "barrio" experience—places like Núñez, Villa Crespo, Balvanera, Once—connected to a humbler experience, they're enchanting.

How would you dress the porteños?

If it were up to me, they'd dress like characters who inhabit the real city and the other city—the fantastical one. The literary one. Free and happy, but evocative of melancholy and Freudian times past. Magical realism with a bit of pepper from the Orient and sea salt from the Mediterranean.

What about flea markets for some treasure hunting?

I normally go to *Feria de Anticuarios* at Barrancas train station in San Isidro, where the Tren de la Costa stops. I also love the *Feria de San Telmo*, the flea market *El Mercado de las Pulgas* on Dorrego and Niceto Vega, plus secondhand clothing sales at *Cottolengo Don Orione* and the *Ejército de Salvación*.

What does the perfect Buenos Aires weekend look like?

A morning walk through San Telmo—I love the covered market. There's a well curated antique shop there called *Gil Antigüedades*, and others on Defensa street. Then to Costanera Sur at noon, where you find the *Reserva Ecológica*. Spend the afternoon walking there.

Then go for a beer at *El Obrero*, in La Boca. At nighttime, dinner at *Tegui* and then dancing at *Tequila*. On Sunday, Zona Norte. Take the train from Belgrano C to Tigre. Before boarding take a stroll through Chinatown to buy some supplies for a picnic at *Casa China*. Get off at Tigre station and hop on the regular bus boats to the Paraná Delta. Once there, any pier next to an uninhabited house can set the stage for a day by the dulce de leche-coloured mirror of water.

What about for urban architecture?

Plaza Francia and the area around the cemetery of course. I'd recommend Mario Roberto Alvarez's building on Schiaffino and Posadas streets, the Palacio Duhau and the Nunciatura Apostólica. Go down Arroyo street and ogle the historical architecture until Plaza San Martín. From there, enjoy the Kavanagh building and the Jacarandá trees—in November their flowers are as blue as the Buenos Aires sky.

What other designers would you like to see gain more recognition?

One project I've loved for years that I'd love to see grow is 12na (12-na.com). It's a collective of Argentines based in Chile, led by Mechi and Mariano. They're geniuses of the paradigm of anti-consumerism and conservation. They're playful—they reuse old clothing to make wonderful pieces. I admire them.

If you could design something for Buenos Aires, what would it be?

I'd design a pen. And I'd give it to everyone who comes to visit. On their way out I'd ask for a copy of all the bar napkins it has scribbled on. Travellers love us and sometimes watch us from the bars. On those squares of paper we might be able to find good ideas to connect Buenos Aires with the world.

Above: Even when the jacarandá trees aren't bedecked in November blue, Plaza San Martín still has a radiant beauty
Below: Around Plaza Dorrego, La Feria de San Telmo has its fair share of peculiar objects and particular characters

A Feast of Senses

It might have been up-and-coming once, but now it's truly up and come. Terrain of late nights, shopping sprees and excellent restaurants, the heart of Buenos Aires' outward-looking side is filled with treasures

Food | The Pick of Picadas

Bodegones in this town are a dime a dozen. And with most, thankfully, there's really no going wrong. The deal is the "picada", essentially a mixed antipasti with chorizo, cheeses, olives and all their delicious ilk, to be picked at along with beer or rough peasant wine. *El Preferido de Palermo* takes this Argentine culinary standby and gives it a Spanish twist, with killer plates of cold cuts and infamous "rabas"—that's fried squid rings—the perfect salty accompaniment to your Quilmes. Aside from providing a delicious pit stop from all the shopping and bar-hopping Palermo's got to offer, the inside of this family-run bar—open since 1952—will probably linger on your brain for a while. Stacked wall-to-wall and floor-to-ceiling with jars, tins, tubs and bottles, this colourful little watering hole is a visual pick-me-up. The restaurant is divided between the canteen and a more serious tablecloth-laden back area, so make sure to pop into the part that has high tables and hanging meats for the full pop-art experience. Served with a copious picada, plenty of drinks and some intense conversation.
• El Preferido de Palermo, Jorge Luis Borges 2108, Palermo

Shop | Don't Call Them Accessories

"They're not dispensable" says *Carla Di Sí* about the handmade glasses sold in her minimalistic showroom (pictured). The retro yet timeless creations, with acetate frames, state they're made by Argentine hands. Meaning they're built to last a lifetime of countless compliments. The same might be said of the shoes at nearby *Mishka*, a favourite among local It Girls. The footwear is crafted from, you guessed it, Argentine leather, and silhouettes are both trend-driven and unique. Quality comes at a price, but then, these non-dispensable mementos will keep giving back.
• Carla Di Sí, Gurruchaga 1677, carladisi.com; Mishka, El Salvador 4673, Palermo, mishka.com.ar

"Cuatro ojos ven más que dos"

Food | Flipping the Grill

After decades of the same Argentine parrilla favourites, a crew of young tattoo-sleeved cooks set out to modernise the righteous grill. *La Carnicería* (pictured) brings creative takes on sweetbreads, blood sausage, chorizos, and massive slabs of smoked grass-fed steaks, all paired with yerba mate-infused gin and tonic. Don't miss *Chori*, the owners' newly opened fast-food place a few blocks away, to try a twist on the country's favourite street food, the "choripán". Here, diners can choose from a handful of sausage sandwiches, each made with a different homemade grilled chorizo on fresh baked bread.
• Palermo, various locations, see Index p.60

Food | Frozen Fans

Just one more result of cultural cross-pollination— the Argentines have taken Italian gelato and made it even better. You can thank the happy, free-roaming cows for that. The scene begs specialist knowledge: think late-night ice cream parlours, where you can buy by the litre, or even call up for delivery to your door. And among the city's myriad "heladerías", *Scannapieco* falls into the mom 'n' pop category, with a loyal following for half a century. If it's hard to choose a flavour, look to the holy grail of dulce de leche. Bonus points for chocolate chips ("granizado").
• Heladería Scannapieco, Avenida Álvarez Thomas 10, Palermo

Night | 69 and Over

Consistently on the cusp, *Niceto Club* doubles as a live house and nightclub. Thursdays see the infamous "Club 69", a wild burlesque show in which godlike performers of all three sexes dance, strip and cavort to a pumping electronic soundtrack. But check the website for a range of musical possibilities: a typical selection might be a celebration of new French electro, a concert from Puerto Rican ska doyenne Mimi Maura, or even a "participative musical tragedy about existential terrorism". It can get hot inside—but it's always worth breaking a sweat.
• Niceto Club, Avenida Niceto Vega 5510, nicetoclub.com

Food | Populist Palate

It's not everyday you find a political-themed restaurant serving noteworthy local cuisine, but when Gonzalo Alderete Pagés took over as owner in 2013, he decided to make *Perón Perón* as popular as the beloved former president and his first lady Eva. Devout followers of all ages pay homage to the memorabilia-covered shrine. And even non-believers find comfort in the food, including house favourites like fried ossobuco empanadas, bowls of meaty "locro" stew, giant milanesas, grilled pacú river fish, and "pastel de papas"—a minced meat and potato pie.
• Perón Perón, Carranza 2225, Palermo

Night | Cups and Codes

Palermo is a safe bet for a proper night out drinking, and secret speakeasies are becoming more than a trend. To enter *Frank's*, clean up nice and visit Facebook for the password beforehand. Only then can you enter through a phone booth. Sister location *Nicky Harrison*, behind Nicky NY Sushi, is even more exclusive. A nice tip in the restaurant might loosen the waiter's tongue about the secret word. Less picky about its patrons, *Rey de Copas* (pictured) is a spectacular bar owned by the son of famed artist Carlos Páez Vilaró. It's set in a hall—spacious, yet romantic—its walls sprinkled with art from the owner's collection.
• Palermo, various locations, see Index p.60

This Old Thing?

Best arrive with a half-empty suitcase because this city's independent fashion scene is thriving locally—meaning lots of the good stuff isn't physically available elsewhere. Starting at your base, *Juana de Arco* adds all the colour and print to underwear and yoga gear. To top it with classic, timeless pieces individualised with curious ruffles and pleats, try *Nous Etudions*. You'll find many of the best-dressed men in town—or Palermo, anyway—are wearing *Hermanos Estebecorena*, while edgier folks might be more at home at *Black Mamba*. *CoraGroppo* does a healthy amount of draped layers, comparable to Ann Demeulemeester, while the Antwerp alumnus behind *House of Matching Colours* (pictured) has returned home to fill her flagship store with incredible pieces she once put on Beyoncé. Older stores shouldn't be avoided either. National chains, though dotted around, still produce stuff that feels unique. *AY Not Dead* do a great job at cool, young fashion, *Rapsodia* make nailing the eclectic boheme look as breezy as it sounds and, for the more structured lady, *Jazmín Chebar* approaches print and embellishment in a very tidy way. For those somewhere in between, *Maria Cher* combines resolved silhouettes with chilled-out fabrication and an unrivalled footwear vision.

• Palermo, various locations, see Index p.60

Julieta Laso, Musician
Un Soplo la Vida

Showing that tango is a living, breathing art form is Julieta, a porteña born in 1982 who came through an acting career to find her voice as a tanguera. She can be found giving her vibrant performances in front of "new tango" powerhouse Orquesta Típica Fernandez Fierro

Buenos Aires has always been a fizzing fountain of alternative culture, and genres continue to be interrogated and blended by the city's bold creative contingent. Julieta brings us to the hidden spots where tango is alive, well and evolving, introduces us to some groundbreaking theatre, and leads us from trendy nightspots to edgy rocker hangouts

How did you end up in the world of tango?

I started working as an actress, and one day my path brought me strongly into tango. What was fundamental was the advice and support of a few great musicians who encouraged me; taking me under their wings. Tango hit me pretty emphatically, I'd even say it was inevitable, and everything seemed natural, as if it had to be that way. Like something you're not looking for, but which finds you.

Is tango still relevant today?

For me, the art itself is either relevant or not, regardless of the genre. And yes I believe there are relevant works in tango today. That's to say there are relevant artists, and genuine and powerful explorations.

Could you describe the tango worlds?

There's a young scene from the rock world, which at some moment spilled into tango. It's full of bands with new compositions. This has developed a lot over the last 15 years, and our orchestra Fernandez Fierro is a key influence in this world of "new tango". Our venue *Club Atletico Fernandez Fierro* is a space where new projects develop; there's an interesting programme from Wednesday to Sunday where much of this can be seen. The surrounding barrio of Almagro is perhaps the most "tanguero" barrio nowadays: with milongas, bars and musicians playing in various spots.

Then, there's also the touristic world, with a kind of tango that for me is more of a show than a humble, genuine form of expression. Let's say it's for export. It's not what I look for, nor choose to watch anywhere.

Where else can we hear good tango?

There are milongas like *La Catedral*, which is both for music and dance. I don't dance—but you can go even if you don't. There's lots of young people, bands play... It's an old mansion with very eccentric décor. Tuesday is when you have to go. And then you can come on Wednesdays to see us. Then, *Torquato Tasso* is a big theatre that only plays tango music. It's the biggest, non-touristy tango theatre, and they have a whole programme.

Are there bars with that vibe?

El Boliche de Roberto is a kind of worker's bar that's very interesting to look at because it's so old, and there's usually some old drunk singing... That's what it is, a bar for drunks and old tango guys. I don't go anymore. It gets so full these days it's hard to even get in there. Otherwise, *Don Narciso* is a new place, a tango bar, in a residential area. Sometimes I go, and just start singing, without letting them know first, or a guitarist and singer could start playing impromptu. A lot of musicians go there. The music is tango, and the place has a tango aesthetic. Further afield is *Bar Los Laureles*. This is a gorgeous place—very old and pretty far away. You wouldn't go there unless you're going specifically. They have tango concerts and milongas. The area is a bit rough, but the place is worth it.

What do you do other than tango?

This city offers many artistic and nocturnal activities—they call it the "la ciudad de la furia" (the city of fury) since it never relaxes and there's so much going on. I like going to the theatre a lot—there's a very interesting and rich scene here.

Where should we start with theatre?

Buenos Aires is famous for all its theatres, and the level is really high. There's a lot of alternative work, and always a massive demand. I really like the work of director

Club Cultural Matienzo offers up a roster of gigs in an intimate venue with good acoustics and a reasonably priced bar

Ricardo Bartís. I go to every play he puts on at his venue, *Sportivo Teatral*. He always uses the same company of actors who understand his aesthetic. It has a lot of dialogue, but he works a lot with physicality and image so you could enjoy it if you don't understand Spanish. Another guy whose work really interests me is Toto Castiñeiras. He always has a few shows going on. He was a clown for Cirque de Soleil, then settled in Buenos Aires. He does fascinating productions and works in some of the many independent theatres.

Where do you listen to other music?
  Club Cultural Matienzo is a great place to have a drink and they always have interesting acts. It's usually pop or alternative. More and more people are going there, it's pretty full these days. Then, there's

Café Vinilo in Palermo. You pay an entrance fee and see a show—you can also eat there. They have an interesting programme.

What about for just plain drinking?
  In Palermo there are bars like *Festival*—it's super trendy, with good cocktails and electronic music playing. Otherwise for the opposite style, try *Nebula*. It's a rocker's bar—it's pretty funny. Very "roots".

Do you have favourite restaurants?
  Perón Perón is a place I like to go to, the food is delicious and they have many traditional Argentine dishes. Plus many options if you like meat. We also have great pizzerías, like *Güerrín* downtown.

What's the best parrilla?
  The best is an asado at my uncle's place or with friends... I don't have

Worth the trip to the barrio of Barracas is Bar Los Laureles, a cultural landmark and home to some serious local tango

a favourite parrilla but a good one in Palermo is *Don Niceto*. It's not fancy at all—it's calm, and it's not the best parrilla in Buenos Aires. But it's popular and the "chinchulines" (intestines) are excellent.

What music would let us get to know the porteño identity?

Tango of course, the old stuff: Carlos Gardel obviously, Osvaldo Pugliese, Edmundo Rivero, Nelly Omar, Troilo, El Polaco Goyeneche, El Tata Floreal Ruiz… It's a long list and I could go on longer. For new tango, apart from our orchestra, there's El Tata Cedrón, Cuarteto la Pua, 34 Puñaladas, Rascasuelos, Cruz Maldonado, Melingo, La Chicana, etc. For folk music, Cuchi Leguizamón, Atahualpa Yupanki, Mercedes Sosa. And for rock, Charly García, Spinetta, Gustavo Cerati, el Indio Solari, and loads more.

Do you write your own tangos?

I'm trying, but I'm not happy with them yet. I like the words I write, but setting them to music is hard. So I'm still working at it.

And where might you go for some inspiration?

I like going around by bike. Last time I went to the *Reserva Ecológica*. I also like travelling around the Province of Buenos Aires, places like Ramos Mejía and Avellaneda—we've been playing a few gigs out there recently. It's interesting what you can see when you're far from the city, the landscapes… My family are close to Ezeiza in the countryside, and I go every so often. That place does me good.

Cambalache

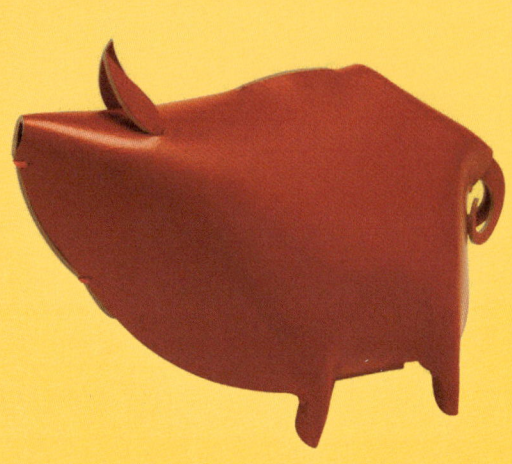

Nose to Tail

Vacavaliente's creations give the countless odds and ends left behind by the local leather industry a colourful new lease on life. Which places these cheery desktop organisers at the sparsely inhabited intersection of form, function and sustainability.
• Chancho (pig), vacavaliente.com

Milonga-ready

When two friends set out to create shoes for their beloved tango, they didn't expect their designs to become as ubiquitous as they did. Known for the trademark flower appliqués, Gretaflora's shoes will put you in sync with the River Plate's sultriest steppers.
• Amalia, gretaflora.com

Pagan Power

"When my innocent blood, spilled, reaches God—I will return as favours for my people." Patron saint of truck drivers and wayward souls, the most Argentine of martyrs is truly one for the people. Find him in altars around most neighbourhoods, on city buses and along every road leading out into the country.
• Gauchito Gil, Santería Belén, santeriabelen.com.ar

Books

On Heroes and Tombs
• Ernesto Sábato, 1961

Sábato's magnum opus, frequently cited as one of the century's great novels, presents a search for identity and a clash of old and new, amid a vividly depicted Buenos Aires. The author quit his career as a radiation physicist to dedicate himself to literature, and his existentialist style was praised by Camus himself.

Hopscotch
• Julio Cortázar, 1963

This wild modernist masterpiece could hardly be described as light reading, but it's also rewarding for its intellectual playfulness and sensory abandon. Hop between the avant-garde scenes of 1960s Paris and Buenos Aires as you literally hop between the chapters of the book—in one of two sequences offered by the author.

My Heart Flooded With Water: Selected Poems
• Alfonsina Storni, 2009

This bilingual collection of poems by one of Latin America's most inspirational women spans 20 years of fatally beautiful work, including her last poem "I'm Going To Sleep", written before she waded to her death in the Río de la Plata.

Films

Wild Tales
• Damián Szifrón, 2014

Social satire hums through six integrated short films, each exploring the eye-watering extremes of human behaviour. Brilliant enough for the Oscar nomination but too edgy to win it—moments will stay with you.

The Blonds
• Albertina Carri, 2003

Argentina's brutal dictatorship of 1974-1983 saw tens of thousands of people "disappeared" by the state. This film—part documentary, part reconstruction—follows the director's search for the story of her parents, victims of the "Dirty War".

Nine Queens
• Fabián Bielinsky, 2000

Nobody hustles better than the porteños—see it play out in this engrossing crime caper that makes "Lock Stock" look like child's play. Enjoy the razor-sharp Buenos Aires repartee, and a star turn by the always excellent Ricardo Darín.

Music

Segundo
• Juana Molina, 2000

Molina achieved success in the US, Europe and even Japan before her homeland. This album inspired David Byrne to bring her along on tour, and is a good starting point for getting lost in her haunting vocals and looping-pedal wizadry.

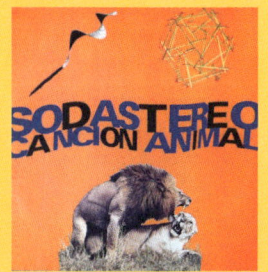

Canción Animal
• Soda Stereo, 1990

This three-piece group, fronted by the late, great Gustavo Cerati, was formed in oversaturated, under-rated basements of Buenos Aires, and became one of the continent's greatest rock exports ever. And on this breakthrough album, there is not a single unnecessary note.

Tango: Zero Hour
• Astor Piazzolla, 1988

About as far from the traditional tango parlour as "The White Album" is from Chuck Berry, Piazzolla transformed the genre into a scintillating universe. Hear the genius composer play his own bandoneón on what he considered to be his greatest album—and the culmination of a staggering career.

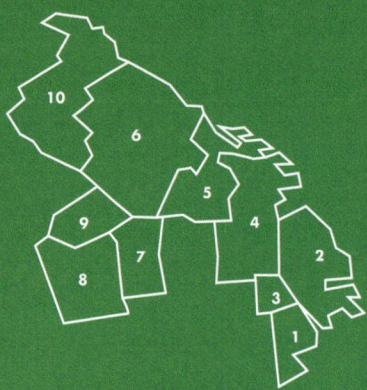

1/ La Boca

El Obrero
Agustín R. Caffarena 64
+54 11 4362-9912
→ p.11, 48 F

Fundación Proa
Avenida Don Pedro de Mendoza 1929
proa.org → p.11 C

Il Matterello Ristorante
Martín Rodríguez 517
+54 11 4307-0529
→ p.31 F

Isla Flotante
Avenida Don Pedro de Mendoza 1561
galeriaislaflotante.com.ar → p.11 C

La Bombonera
Brandsen 805
bocajuniors.com
→ p.8 L

Usina del Arte
Agustín R. Caffarena 1
usinadelarte.org
→ p.11 C

2/ Puerto Madero

Reserva Ecológica Costanera Sur
→ p.16, 48, 57 L

Happening
Avenida Alicia Moreau de Justo 310
+54 11 4319-8712
happening.com.ar
→ p.33 F

3/ San Telmo

Amorinda
Defensa 677
+54 11 4331-3236
amorinda.com.ar
→ p.24 F

Café San Juan La Cantina
Chile 474
+54 11 4300-9344
→ p.24 F

Feria de San Telmo
Defensa 1098
feriadesantelmo.com
→ p.48 S

Garage Bar
Chile 631
+54 11 6091-1354
→ p.24 N

Gil Antigüedades
Humberto Primo 412
+54 11 4361-5019
gilantiguedades.com.ar → p.48 S

Gran Parrilla del Plata
Chile 594
+54 11 4300-8858
parrilladelplata.com.ar → p.11 F

Jhabibi Cocina Árabe
Humberto Primo 527
+54 11 4300-7172
→ p.23 F

La Carretería
Avenida Brasil 656
+54 11 4300-5564
lacarreteria.jimdo.com
→ p.23 F

Nuestra Parilla
Carlos Calvo 471
→ p.11 F

Torquato Tasso
Defensa 1575
torquatotasso.com.ar
→ p.55 C

4/ Centro

Banchero
Av. Corrientes 1300
→ p.23 F

Bebop Club
Moreno 364
bebopclub.com.ar
→ p.25 N

Café Tortoni
Avenida de Mayo 825
cafetortoni.com.ar
→ p.33 F

Celta Bar
Sarmiento 1701
54 11 4371-7338
→ p.24 F

Chiquilín de Bachín
Sarmiento 1599
+54 11 4373-5163
chiquin.com.ar
→ p.23 F

Cocoliche
Av. Rivadavia 878
→ p.8 N

El Palacio de la Papa Frita
Av. Corrientes 1612
elpalaciodelapapafrita.com
→ p.23 F

Florería Atlántico
Arroyo 872
+54 11 4313-6093
floreriaatlantico.com.ar → p.32 N

Fundación Federico Jorge Klemm
M. T. de Alvear 628
fundacionfjklemm.org
→ p.24 C

La Casa de la Cultura
Av. de Mayo 575
+54 11 4323-9669
→ p.16 C

La Paz
Av. Corrientes 1593
+54 11 4373-3647
→ p.24 F

Los Galgos
Avenida Callao 501
+54 11 4371-3561
barlosgalgos.com.ar
→ p.24, 31 N

Los Inmortales
Av. Corrientes 1369
losinmortales.com
→ p.23 F

Parrilla Peña
Rodríguez Peña 682
+54 11 4371-5643
parrillapenia.url.ph
→ p.11 F

Pizzería Güerrín
Av. Corrientes 1368
pizzeriaguerrin.com
→ p.23, 56 F

Rotisería Miramar
Av. San Juan 1999
+54 11 4304-4261
→ p.14 F

5/ Recoleta

Biblioteca Nacional Mariano Moreno
Agüero 2502
bn.gov.ar → p.16 C

DIVING HEADFIRST INTO WHAT MAKES EACH CITY ITS OWN

LOST iN

The City

Getting lost in the city is not about throwing away the map
It's about surrendering yourself to the essence of the place
The art and creativity that provide its individual inspiration
The sights, smells, flavours and sounds that make it unique

Cementerio de
la Recoleta
Junín 1760 → p.46 Ⓛ

Fervor
Posadas 1519
fervorbrasas.com.ar
→ p.47 Ⓕ

Mite
Av. Santa Fe 2729
mitegaleria.com.ar
→ p.16 Ⓒ

Museo de Arquitectura
y Diseño (MARQ)
Av. del Libertador 999
socearq.org → p.47 Ⓒ

Museo Nacional
de Bellas Artes
Avenida del
Libertador 1473
mnba.gob.ar
→ p.24, 47 Ⓒ

Museo Xul Solar
Laprida 1212
xulsolar.org.ar
→ p.16 Ⓒ

Notorious
Avenida Callao 966
notorious.com.ar
→ p.25 Ⓝ

Sottovoce
Avenida del
Libertador 1098
+54 11 4807-6691
sottovoce.com.ar
→ p.47 Ⓕ

Tramando
Rodríguez Peña 1973
tramando.com
→ p.46 Ⓢ

6/ Palermo

AY Not Dead
Gurruchaga 1637 (W),
1715 (M)
aynotdead.com.ar
→ p.53 Ⓢ

BlackMamba
Soler 4502
beblackmamba.com
→ p.53 Ⓢ

Bosques De Palermo
Av. Infanta Isabel 410
→ p.7, 48 Ⓛ

Carla Di Sí
Gurruchaga 1677
carladisi.com.ar
→ p.51 Ⓢ

Casa Cavia
Cavia 2985
casacavia.com
→ p.10 Ⓕ

Chicco Ruiz – DAM
Thames 1780
→ p.14 Ⓢ

Chori
Thames 1653
+54 11 3966-9857
→ p.51 Ⓕ

CoraGroppo
El Salvador 4657
coragroppo.com
→ p.53 Ⓢ

Don Julio
Guatemala 4699
+54 11 4832-6058
parrilladonjulio.com.ar
→ p.11, 31 Ⓕ

Don Niceto
Avenida Coronel
Niceto Vega 5255
+54 11 4777-8534
→ p.57 Ⓕ

Dubié
República de
la India 3139
dubie.com
→ p.14 Ⓢ

El Preferido de
Palermo
Jorge Luis Borges 2108
+54 11 4774-6585
→ p.50 Ⓕ

Festival
Gorriti 5741
+54 11 4775-6733
→ p.56 Ⓝ

Frank's
Arévalo 1443
+54 11 4777-6541
→ p.33, 52 Ⓝ

Gran Dabbang
Avenida Scalabrini
Ortiz 1543
+54 11 4832-1186
→ p.31 Ⓕ

Heladería
Scannapieco
Av. Álvarez Thomas 10
+54 11 4777-3528
→ p.33, 51 Ⓕ

Hermanos
Estebecorena
El Salvador 5960
+54 11 4772-2145
hermanos
estebecorena.com
→ p.53 Ⓢ

Home Hotel
Honduras 5860
+54 11 4779-1006
homebuenosaires.com
→ p.15 Ⓛ

House of Matching
Colours
Cabello 3843
houseofmatching
colours.com → p.53 Ⓢ

Jazmín Chebar
El Salvador 4702
→ p.53 Ⓢ

Juana de Arco
El Salvador 4762
juanadearco.net
→ p.53 Ⓢ

La Carnicería
Thames 2317
+54 11 2071-7199
→ p.51 Ⓕ

La Mar
Arévalo 2024
+54 11 4776 5543
lamarcebicheria.
com.ar → p.14 Ⓕ

M
El Salvador 5783
+54 11 4331-3879
mbuenosaires.com.ar
→ p.25 Ⓕ

María Cher
El Salvador 4724
maria-cher.com.ar
→ p.53 Ⓢ

Mishiguene
Lafinur 3368
+54 11 3969-0764
mishiguene.com
→ p.32 Ⓕ

Mishka
El Salvador 4673
mishka.com.ar
→ p.51 Ⓢ

MALBA
Av. F. Alcorta 3415
malba.org.ar
→ p.24, 47 Ⓒ

Museo Evita
Lafinur 2988
museoevita.org
→ p.24 Ⓒ

Museo Nacional
de Arte Decorativo
Avenida del
Libertador 1902
mnad.org → p.47 Ⓒ

Niceto Club
Av. Coronel Niceto
Vega 5510
nicetoclub.com
→ p.52 Ⓝ

Nicky Harrison
Malabia 1764
nicky-harrison.com
→ p.52 Ⓝ

Nous Etudions
Armenia 1933
nousetudions.com
→ p.53 Ⓢ

Panorama Store
República de la
India 2905 → p.10 Ⓢ

Patrón
Malabia 1644
patronba.com
→ p.10 Ⓢ

Perón Perón
Ángel Carranza 2225
+54 11 4777-6194
→ p.52, 56 Ⓕ

Planetario Galileo
Galilei
Avenida Sarmiento
planetario.gov.ar
→ p.7 Ⓒ

Proper
Aráoz 1676
+54 11 4831-0027
properbsas.com.ar
→ p.31 Ⓕ

Rapsodia Palermo
Viejo
Honduras 4874
rapsodia.com
→ p.53 Ⓢ

Rey de Copas
Gorriti 5176
reydecopasbar.com
→ p.52 Ⓝ

Sportivo Teatral
Thames 1426
sportivoteatral.com.ar
→ p.56 Ⓒ

Tegui
Costa Rica 5852
+54 11 4770-9500
tegui.com.ar
→ p.31, 48 Ⓕ

Tequila
Av. Costanera Norte
and La Pampa
→ p.48 Ⓝ

Café Vinilo
Gorriti 3780
cafevinilo.com.ar
→ p.56 Ⓝ

7/ Almagro

Café El Banderín
Guardia Vieja 3601
+54 11 4862-7757
elbanderin.com.ar
→ p.21 Ⓕ

Club Atlético Fernández Fierro
Sánchez de Bustamante 772
caff.com.ar
→ p.25, 55 Ⓝ

El Boliche de Roberto
Bulnes 331
+54 11 4862-0415
→ p.21, 55 Ⓝ

La Catedral
Sarmiento 4006
lacatedralclub.com
→ p.21, 55 Ⓝ

Ladran Sancho
Guardia Vieja 3811
+54 11 4863-1095
→ p.20 Ⓕ

Las Violetas
Av. Rivadavia 3899
+54 11 4958-7387
lasvioletas.com
→ p.20 Ⓕ

Pierino
Lavalle 3499
+54 11 4864-5715
lacantinadepierino.
com.ar → p.21 Ⓕ

8/ Caballito

Museo Argentino de Ciencias Naturales
Ángel Gallardo 490
macn.gov.ar
→ p.19, 24 Ⓒ

Parque Centenario
Avenida Patricias
Argentinas → p.19 Ⓛ

9/ Villa Crespo

Angelín
Av. Córdoba 5270
+54 11 4774-3836
→ p.23 Ⓕ

Bar 878
Thames 878
+54 11 4773-1098
878bar.com.ar
→ p.20, 24 Ⓝ

Club Cultural Matienzo
Pringles 1249
+54 11 6610-1520
ccmatienzo.com.ar
→ p.56 Ⓝ

Gachi Prieto
Uriarte 1976
gachiprietogallery.com
→ p.18 Ⓒ

Hache
Loyola 32
hachegaleria.com
→ p.16 Ⓒ

I Latina
Murillo 725
+54 11 4857-9095
ilatinabuenosaires.
com → p.19 Ⓕ

JT
Humboldt 291
jtbyjt.com → p.20 Ⓢ

La Internacional Argentina
Padilla 865
+54 11 2070-4939
→ p.15 Ⓢ

La Ira de Dios
Aguirre 1029
lairadedios.com.ar
→ p.18 Ⓒ

La Mamma Rosa
Jufré 202
+54 11 4773-2913
→ p.19 Ⓕ

Librería Punc
Doctor Luis
Beláustegui 393
→ p.15 Ⓢ

Nébula
Serrano 1160
+54 11 4777-0433
→ p.56 Ⓝ

Nora Fisch
Av. Córdoba 5222
norafisch.com → p.18 Ⓒ

Ruth Benzacar
J. R. de Velasco 1287
ruthbenzacar.com
→ p.18 Ⓒ

Slyzmud
Bonpland 721
slyzmud.com
→ p.18 Ⓒ

Yeite
Humboldt 293
+54 11 4855-6777
→ p.20 Ⓕ

10/ Belgrano & Colegiales

Casa China
Arribeños 2173
+54 11 4786-1142
casachina.info
→ p.48 Ⓕ

El Mercado de las Pulgas
Avenida Dorrego 1650
→ p.48 Ⓢ

Formosa Galería
Delgado 1235
→ p.16 Ⓒ

Hong Kong Style
+54 11 4786-3456
Montañeses 2149
→ p.32 Ⓕ

Museo de Arte Español Enrique Larreta
Juramento 2291
+54 11 4783-2640
→ p.15 Ⓛ

Parque de la Memoria
Costanera Norte
→ p.16 Ⓛ

Sucre
Mariscal Antonio José
de Sucre 676
sucrerestaurant.com.ar
→ p.31 Ⓕ

11/ Tigre

Club de Regatas la Marina
Paseo Victorica
crlm.org.ar → p.9 Ⓛ

Estación Fluvial Gral. Bartolomé
Mitre 305
+54 11 4512-4497
→ p.9 Ⓛ

Museo de Arte Tigre
Av. Victorica 972
+54 11 4512-4528
mat.gov.ar → p.9 Ⓛ

Puerto de Frutos
Sarmiento 160
wp.puertodefrutos-
arg.com.ar → p.9 Ⓢ

12/ Other

Bar Los Laureles
Avenida General
Iriarte 2290, Barracas
+54 11 4303-3393
barloslaureles.com.ar
→ p.55 Ⓝ

Cottolengo Don Orione
Av. Pte A Illia 4250,
San Miguel
+54 11 4664-6796
→ p.48 Ⓢ

Don Narciso Almacén
Camarones 1645,
Villa General Mitre
+54 11 5249-3403
→ p.55 Ⓝ

Ejército de Salvación
Avenida Sáenz 580,
Nueva Pompeya
ejercitodesalvacion.
org.ar → p.48 Ⓢ

El Ferroviario
Avenida Reservistas
Argentinos 219, Liniers
+54 11 4644-2360
→ p.11 Ⓕ

El Monumental
Av. Pres. Figueroa
Alcorte 7597, Núñez
cariverplate.com.ar
→ p.8 Ⓛ

Espacio Memoria y Derechos Humanos (ESMA)
Avenida del Libertador
8151, Núñez
+54 11 4702 9920
espaciomemoria.ar
→ p.16 Ⓒ

Estadio José Amalfitani
Av. Juan B. Justo 900,
Liniers
velezsarsfield.com.ar
→ p.8 Ⓛ

Estadio Libertadores de America
R. E. Bochini 951,
Avellaneda
clubaindependiente.
com → p.8 Ⓛ

Feria de Anticuarios
Tren de la Costa 735,
San Isidro
delanticuario.com
→p.48 Ⓢ

Reserva Ecológica Vicente López
La Lucila
→p.16 Ⓛ

Also available from LOST iN

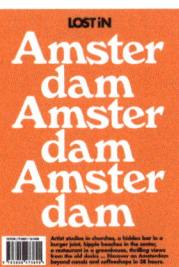

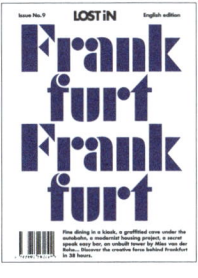

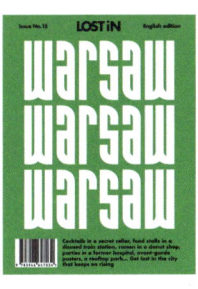

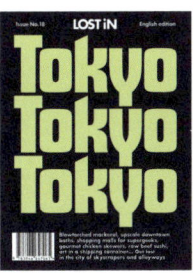

LOSTIN.COM

El Hombre Sirena

Samanta Schweblin

Story

The Merman

Samanta Schweblin

I'm sitting at the harbour café, waiting for Daniel, when I see the merman looking at me from the dock. He's on the first concrete pillar, where the water doesn't reach, about 50 metres away. It takes me a while to understand what he is exactly: so much of a man waist up, so much of a siren waist down. He looks off to one side, then calmly in the other direction, and in the end looks back here again. But I know the café owner is Daniel's friend, and he's watching me from the bar. I pretend to be searching on the table for the bill, as if I've suddenly just decided to leave. The owner comes over to see if everything's okay; he insists that I should stay, that Daniel is about to arrive, that I should wait for him. I tell him to relax, I'll be back soon. I leave five pesos on the table, take my handbag, and go. I don't have a plan for the merman: I just leave the café and walk in his direction. Contrary to our idea that mermaids are gorgeous and tanned, this one is not only of the other sex, but also quite pasty. Still, he's solid, muscular. When he sees me he crosses his arms—hands under armpits, thumbs upward—and smiles. It seems a bit too cocky for a merman and I regret walking towards him with so much certainty, so keen to talk to him, and I feel stupid. But it's too late to go back. He waits for me to get closer and says:

"Hey."

I stop.

"What's a beauty like you doing all alone at the docks?"

"I thought maybe..."—I don't know what to say. I let my handbag fall, holding it with both hands, hanging it in front of my knees, like a little girl—"I thought maybe I needed something, like your good self..."

"Don't be so formal, gorgeous" he says, and takes my hand, to help me up.

I look at his legs, or rather, his sparkling tail hanging over the concrete. I pass him my handbag. He takes it and places it next to him. I stick a foot onto the dock and take the hand. His skin is icy, like frozen fish. But the sun is high and strong, the sky is intense blue and the air smells clean, and when I settle next to him I feel as if the coldness of his body is filling me with a vitalising happiness. I feel embarrassed and pull loose. I don't

know what to do with my hands. I smile. He fixes his hair—an American-style quiff—and asks if I have cigarettes. I say I don't smoke. He has smooth skin: there's not a single hair on his whole body and it's covered with tiny rings of white dust, hardly visible, perhaps from the sea salt. He sees me looking and brushes off a bit from his arms. His abs are defined; I've never seen a stomach like it.

"You can touch me," he says, caressing his abs. "You wouldn't find anything like this downtown, would you?"

I reach out a hand, he brings it closer and imprisons it between his hand and his abs, which are also freezing. He keeps me there for a few seconds, and then says:

"Tell me about yourself"—he lets me go smoothly —"How is everything?"

"Mama is sick, the doctors say she's going to die soon."

We both look at the sea.

"That's awful..." he says.

"But that's not the problem," I say, "I'm more worried about Daniel. Daniel's not doing well and that doesn't help."

"Does he find it hard to accept his mother's situation?"

I nod.

"There's two of you?"

"Yes."

"At least you can share it. I'm an only child and my mother is suffocating."

"There's two of us, but he does everything. I need to be relaxed, I can't allow myself strong emotions. I have a problem here, in the heart, I think it's the heart. So I keep a distance. For my health..."

"And where's Daniel now?"

"He's always late. He spends the whole day running around. He has a big problem with organising his time."

"What's his sign? Leo?"

"Taurus."

"Uff! What a sign."

"I've got mints," I say, "do you want one?"

He says yes and passes my handbag, which was still on his side.

"He thinks the whole day about where he's going to find the money to pay for this and that. All the time wanting to know what I'm doing, where I'm going to be, with who..."

"Does he live with your mother?"

"No, Mama is like me, we're independent women and need our space. He thinks it's dangerous for me to live alone. He says it just like that: 'I think it's dangerous for a girl like you to live alone'. He wants to pay for a maid to follow me around all day long. Of course I haven't accepted."

I pass him a mint and take one for me.

"Do you live around here?"

"He rents a little house for me a few blocks away: he thinks this neighbourhood is much safer. And he's made friends around here, he speaks to the neighbours, the bar owner—he wants to know everything, control everything. It's really unbearable."

"My father was like that."

"Yes, but he's not Papa. Papa is dead. Why do I have to put up with another Papa when Papa is dead?"

"Well, maybe he just wants to look after you."

I laugh, but sarcastically—his comment almost ruins my mood, and I think he notices.

"No, no. He doesn't try to look after me, it's more complicated than you think."

He looks at me. He has blue eyes, very light.

"Tell me."

"Ah, no. Believe me, it's not worth it: it's a beautiful day."

"Please"

He presses his palms together and begs with a funny face, like an angel about to cry. Sometimes when he talks to me, the points of his silver flipper wave and brush my ankles. They're rough, but the scales don't hurt—it's a pleasant sensation. I say nothing, and the flipper gets closer and closer.

"Tell me..."

"It's Mama... She's not just sick: the truth is that the poor thing is completely crazy..."

I breathe and look at the sky. The blue sky: absolute. Then we look at each other. For the first time I notice his lips. Are they also freezing? He takes my hands, kisses them and says:

"Do you think we could go out? You and me, one of these days... We could go for dinner, or to the cinema, I love the cinema."

I give him a kiss and I feel the coldness of his mouth waking up every cell of my body, like an icy drink at the height of summer. It's not just a feeling, it's a revelation, because I feel nothing will ever be the same again. But I can't tell him I love him: not yet, more time has

to pass, we have to take things step by step. First him to the cinema, then me to the bottom of the sea. But I've made a decision, irrevocably, that nothing will ever separate me from him. I—who spent my whole life believing we live for one love—I found mine on the docks, by the sea, and now he takes my hand sincerely, and looks at me with his transparent eyes, and tells me:

"You can stop your suffering, beautiful. Nobody's going to hurt you any more."

A car horn sounds in the distance, from the street. I recognise it immediately: it's Daniel's car. I look over the shoulder of my merman. Daniel gets out in a hurry and goes directly to the café. He doesn't seem to have seen me.

"Back in a moment," I say.

He hugs me, kisses me again, "I'll wait for you," he says, and he offers me his arm as a rope so I can get down easier.

I run to the café. Daniel is talking to the owner and sees me. He looks relieved.

"Where were you? We were supposed to meet at your house, not the café."

That's not true, but I don't say anything. It doesn't matter now.

"I need to talk to you," I say.

"Let's go to the car, we'll talk in the car."

He takes my arm, delicately, but with that paternal attitude that annoys me so much, and we leave. The car is a few metres away, but I stop.

"Let me go."

He lets me go, but keeps on to the car and opens the door.

"Let's go, it's late. The doctor's going to kill us."

"I'm not going anywhere, Daniel."

Daniel pauses.

"I'm staying here," I say, "with the merman."

He stares at me for a moment. I turn around to the sea. He, gorgeous and silver on the dock, waves his arm at us. Daniel, as if he's finally emerged from his trance, gets into the car and opens the door on my side. Then, I don't know what to do, and when I don't know what to do, the world seems a terrible place for some-one like me, and I feel very sad. That's why I think: it's only a merman, it's only a merman, while I get into the car and try to calm down. He could be there again tomorrow, waiting for me.

Samanta Schweblin was born in Buenos Aires in 1978. Her books have been translated into more than 20 languages and won multiple awards, and she's been published in international magazines such as "Granta"

On The Road

The perfect companion for your city trip.

GET THE APP

Access thousands of handpicked locations from your phone.
Download our free app on lostin.com/app

@lostincityguides